Leserabe
First Reading

Marjorie Weinman Sharmat

Nate the Great goes Undercover

Pictures by Detlef Kersten

Ravensburger Buchverlag

Bibliografische Information Der Deutschen Bibliothek:

Die Deutsche Bibliothek verzeichnet diese Publikation
in der Deutschen Nationalbibliografie.
Detaillierte bibliografische Daten sind im Internet
über **http://dnb.ddb.de** abrufbar.

**Die Schreibweise entspricht den Regeln
der neuen Rechtschreibung.**

3 2 1 04 05 06

Die amerikanische Originalausgabe erschien
unter dem Titel „Nate the Great goes Undercover"
bei Coward-McCann, New York

Ravensburger Leserabe

Umschlagbild: Detlef Kersten
Umschlagkonzeption: Sabine Reddig
Printed in Germany
ISBN 3-473-36031-7

www.ravensburger.de
www.leserabe.de

I, Nate the Great, am a detective.
I work hard, I rest hard.
Tonight I am resting hard
from my last case.

It was my first night case.
It started in the morning
before breakfast.
I was walking my dog, Sludge.
Sludge is my new dog.

I found him in a field
eating a stale pancake.
I love pancakes.
I knew he was my kind of dog.

I saw Oliver come
out of his house.
Oliver lives next door.
Sludge and I walked faster.

Oliver walked faster.
Oliver caught up with us.
He always catches up with us.
Oliver is a pest.

"There is a garbage snatcher
in the neighborhood," Oliver said.
"Our can is tipped over every night.
I need help."
Oliver knows I am a detective.
He knows I am a good detective.
"I will help you," I said.
"I, Nate the Great, will help you
pick up your garbage."
"That is not the kind of help
I need," Oliver said.
"I want to know who is taking
the garbage every night."
"That is easy," I said.
"Somebody hungry is taking
your garbage.
Somebody very hungry.

And sleepy.
Somebody sleepy
from getting up every night
to take your garbage."
"Do you know anybody
hungry and sleepy?" Oliver asked.
"Yes," I said. "Me.
I will find the garbage snatcher
after I eat breakfast."

Sludge and I went home.
I cooked a giant pancake.
I gave some to Sludge.

Then we went outside.
I said to Sludge,
"I'll ask questions
while you sniff. If you sniff any
garbage smells, let me know."

I saw Rosamond coming
down the street with her cats.
Rosamond did not look
hungry or sleepy.
She looked
like she always looks.
Strange.

Sludge sniffed while I spoke.
"Rosamond, do you eat garbage?"
Rosamond said, "There are
two thousand other things
I would eat
before I would eat garbage.
First, I would eat hamburger,
ice cream, candy, pickles, bananas,
potato chips, Krispy Krappies,
relish, doughnuts, spaghetti,
ice cubes, mint leaves…"
Rosamond kept talking.

I did not have time
to hear her list
of two thousand things.
I walked on.

Rosamond was still talking.
"Pretzels, artichokes,
baked beans, chocolate pudding,
vegetable soup, walnuts. . ."
Rosamond had two thousand
reasons for not
taking Oliver's garbage.
But what about her cats?

I went back to Rosamond.
"Cauliflower, wafers, lamb chops,"
she said. "Peanuts, egg salad. . . "
"Excuse me," I said.
"Do your cats eat garbage?"
"No," Rosamond said. "My cats
eat cat food, cheese, tuna fish,
milk, salmon pie, liver loaf. . . "
I walked away.

I decided to look for Esmeralda.
Esmeralda always has
her mouth open.
She is either hungry
or about to yawn.
I saw her sitting
in front of her house.
Sludge sniffed. I spoke.
“Do you get up
at night to visit
Oliver’s garbage can?” I asked.
“I would never visit anything
that belongs to Oliver,”
Esmeralda said.
“He might follow me.”
Now I knew why Esmeralda
keeps her mouth open.

She has wise things to say.
She had given me
an important clue.
No person would go near
Oliver or his garbage.
Oliver is too much of a pest.
Sludge and I went home.
Oliver came over.
Oliver always comes over.
Sludge sniffed Oliver.
I gave Sludge a pancake.
"Is the case solved?" Oliver asked.
"Part of it," I said.
"Which part?" he asked.

“I, Nate the Great, have found out
who did **not** take your garbage.
A person did not
take your garbage.”

"Well, who took it?" Oliver asked.
"That is the part
that is not solved," I said.
"I, Nate the Great, say
that an animal or bird took it.
An animal or bird
that goes out
in the night.
I will find out what
and I will be back."

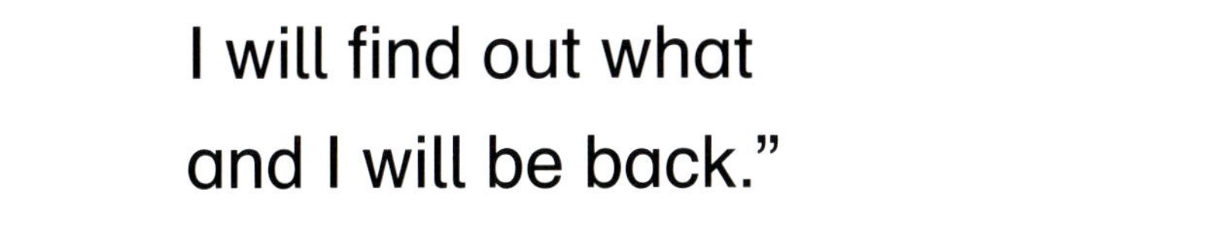

Sometimes I, Nate the Great,
need help.
I went to the library.
I read about birds
that go out in the night.
They are called Strigiformes
and Caprimulgiformes.
I wrote the names down.
Then I crossed them out.

Birds with names like that
would not eat anything
called garbage.
Then I read about cats, rats, bats,
mice, shrews, skunks, raccoons,
opossums, and moles.
They all go out at night.

I read about what they like
and what they do not like.
Then I went home.
Oliver came over.
I said, “A cat, rat, bat, mouse, shrew, skunk, raccoon, opossum, or mole is taking your garbage.”
“Which one?” Oliver asked.
“I don’t know. But tonight, I, Nate the Great, will find out.”

I left a note for my mother.

Dear mother,

I am sleeping out tonight.

I am taking a blanket.

I am taking pancakes.

I will be back.

Love,

Nate the Great

I went out into the yard.
It was cold out there.
I asked Sludge if I could share
his doghouse.
I crawled in.
Sludge crawled out.

It was a small doghouse.
I looked out the window
of the doghouse.
I could not see
Oliver's garbage can.
I crawled out of the doghouse.
I left Sludge a pancake.

Where could I hide?
I, Nate the Great,
knew where to hide.
In the garbage can.
I was sorry I knew.

Detective work is not
fun and games.

Detective work is dirty garbage
cans instead of clean beds.
Detective work is banana peels,
dishrags, milk cartons,
floor sweepings, cigar ashes, fleas,
and me all together in one can.
I peeked out
from under the cover.
The street was quiet.
Then I heard a sound.

Crunch! Crackle! Klunk!

The sound was close to me.

The sound was me.

The garbage can was crunchy
and crackly and klunky.
Every time I moved
it was crunchier and cracklier.
I lifted up the cover. I got out.
I had a new plan. A better plan.
I would not wait
for the garbage snatcher.
I would go out and find him.
I crept down the street.
I looked to the right
and to the left
and behind me.
Right, left, behind.
Right, left, behind.
Smack!

Something big hit me.
It was in front of me.
The one place I forgot to look.

I do not think I made a dent
in the telephone pole.
I kept creeping and looking.
Right, left, behind, front.
Right, left, behind, front.
I came to a field.
Animals like fields.

I saw an animal.

I, Nate the Great, was in luck.

I crept closer

I, Nate the Great, was in bad luck.

It was a skunk.

I started to walk backward.
I saw some stuff on the ground
next to the skunk.
It looked like garbage.
I walked forward to see.
I saw some garbage.
The skunk saw me.
The skunk stamped his feet.
He raised his tail.

I, Nate the Great,
did not run fast enough.
But the case was solved.
The skunk
was the garbage snatcher.
I went home.
I wrote a note to Oliver.
I put it in his mailbox.

Dear Oliver,

I, Nate the Great, have found out
who took your garbage.
It was a skunk.
I, Nate the Great,
know how to get rid of
a skunk.
Put a can of mothballs
next to your garbage can.
Skunks do not like the smell of
mothballs.
I learned this in the Library.
I do not like the smell of skunks.
I learned this in the field.
Yours truly,

Nate the Great

It was not morning yet.
But I knew there was something
I must do right away.

I was glad the water was hot.
In fact, that is how
I spent most of the next day.

The following morning
Oliver came over.
“The case is unsolved,” he said.
“The garbage can is tipped again.”
“Impossible,” I said.
“Come and see
my garbage,” Oliver said.
I, Nate the Great, have had
better invitations.

But I went.
The can was tipped, all right.
“And here is the can of mothballs,”
Oliver said. “
So who is the garbage snatcher?”
he asked.

"I, Nate the Great, will find out,
no matter how long
or how many baths it takes."
I walked away.
Sludge followed me.
He was doing a lot of sniffing.
But, I, Nate the Great,
had a lot of thinking to do.
I gave Sludge a pancake.
There must be a clue I missed.
Sludge ignored the pancake.
He was thinking, too.
I thought harder.
And harder.

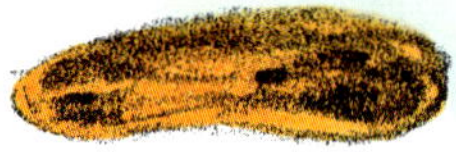

Then I knew what the clue was.
All I needed was the proof.

I left a note for my mother.

I went to the garbage can.
I stepped inside.
I put the cover over me.
I left space to look out
and to breathe.
I knew that was important.
I waited.
Nothing happened.

Something came up to the can.
Something knocked
the cover to the ground.
Something looked inside.
"Something" was Sludge.
Sludge was surprised to see me.
But, I, Nate the Great, had been
expecting to see Sludge.

I knew that Sludge
was the garbage snatcher.
And I knew why.
Sludge was tired of my pancakes.
How could anybody
be tired of pancakes?

Sludge was looking
for his own snack.
Sludge was hungry
I took him back to his doghouse.
I gave him a bone
and a bowl of dog food.

Someday Sludge
will be a great detective,
when he learns to sniff more
and snatch less.
I wanted to take a bath.
But I was too tired.
I wanted to write a note to Oliver.
But I was too tired.
Tomorrow Oliver will come over.
Oliver always comes over.

Now I am resting.
I can hear the sounds of the night.
I can hear the sounds of
a crunchy bone being crunched.
They are good sounds.
My first night case is over.
Maybe it will be
my last night case.
I, Nate the Great, am pooped.

Vokabelverzeichnis

(to) go undercover	verdeckt ermitteln
(to) rest	sich ausruhen
case	Kriminalfall
(to) walk the dog	den Hund spazieren führen
stale	fad, schal
next door	nebenan
(to) catch up	aufholen
a pest	Pest, Nervensäge
garbage	Abfall, Müll
snatcher	Dieb
neighborhood	Nachbarschaft
can	Mülltonne
(to) tip over	umkippen
(to) pick up	aufheben, aufräumen
(to) get up	aufstehen
anybody	irgendeiner, irgendjemand
giant	riesig
while	während
(to) sniff	schnüffeln
(to) smell	riechen, duften
(to) let someone know	jemandem Bescheid geben
strange	sonderbar, komisch
candy	Bonbon, Süßigkeit
pickle	Essiggurke
relish	Würze, Grillsoße
ice cubes	Eiswürfel
mint leaves	Minze
(to) keep doing something	nicht aufhören, etwa zu tun

still	immer noch
pretzel	Brezel
reason	Grund
wafers	Waffeln
lamb chops	Lammkoteletts
Excuse me!	Entschuldigung!
tuna fish	Tunfisch
salmon pie	Lachstorte
liver loaf	Leberkäse
(to) decide	entscheiden
(to) look for	Ausschau halten nach
either ... or	entweder ... oder
(to) yawn	gähnen
anything	irgendetwas
(to) belong to	gehören
may, might	können
(to) keep	beibehalten, halten
clue	Hinweis
(to) come over	bei jmdm. zu Hause vorbeikommen
(to) solve	lösen
library	Bücherei
(to) cross something out	etwas durchstreichen
rat	Ratte
bat	Fledermaus
mice	Mäuse
shrew	Spitzmaus
raccoon	Waschbär
opossum	Beutelratte, Opossum
mole	Maulwurf

(to) leave, left	hinterlassen, lassen
note	Nachricht
blanket	Bettdecke
yard	Hof
(to) share	teilen
(to) crawl	krabbeln
where	wo
(to) hide	verstecken
peel	Pelle
dishrags	Abwaschlappen
floor sweepings	Kehricht, Abfall
fleas	Flöhe
(to) peek	spähen, nachsehen
cover	Deckung
sound	Geräusch
crunchy	knusprig, raschelig
crackly	rissig
(to) lift up	anheben
(to) creep, crept	kriechen, schleichen
(to) hit	treffen
(to) forget, forgot, forgotten	vergessen
dent	Beule
telephone pole	Telefonmast
(to) be in luck	Glück haben
skunk	Stinktier
(to) stamp	stampfen
(to) raise	anheben
tail	Schwanz
mailbox	Briefkasten, Brieffach
(to) get rid of something	etwas loswerden

mothballs	Mottenkugeln
smell	Geruch
yours truly	mit lieben Grüßen
yet	noch
right away	auf der Stelle
(to) be glad	froh sein, sich freuen
in fact	tatsächlich
backward	rückwärts
no matter	ganz gleich
(to) ignore	nicht beachten
proof	Beweis
(to) step inside	eintreten
(to) come up	heraufkommen
(to) knock	schlagen, stoßen
ground	Boden
(to) be tired of	genug haben von
snack	Imbiss
bowl	Schüssel
(to) snatch	rauben, ergattern, fangen
(to) be pooped	ausgepumpt sein